Eve's Striptease

PITT POETRY SERIES
Ed Ochester, Editor

JULIA KASDORF

Eve's Striptease

UNIVERSITY OF PITTSBURGH PRESS

The publication of this book is supported by a grant
from the Pennsylvania Council on the Arts

Published by the University of Pittsburgh Press, Pittsburgh, Pa. 15261

Manufactured in the United States of America

Printed on acid-free paper

10 9 8 7 6 5 4 3 2 1

Library of Congress Cataloging-in-Publication data and acknowledgments
are located at the end of this book.

A CIP catalog record for this book is available from the British Library.

Laughter follows us
falls from us,
the petals from trees
or in autumn, leaves.

Contents

II. MAP OF THE KNOWN WORLD

I

FIRST GESTURES

First Gestures

Among the first we learn is good-bye,
your tiny wrist between Dad's forefinger
and thumb forced to wave bye-bye to Mom,
whose hand sails brightly behind a windshield.
Then it's done to make us follow:
in a crowded mall, a woman waves, "Bye,
we're leaving," and her son stands firm
sobbing, until at last he runs after her,
among shoppers drifting like sharks
who must drag their great hulks
underwater, even in sleep, or drown.

Living, we cover vast territories;
imagine your life drawn on a map—
a scribble on the town where you grew up,
each bus trip traced between school
and home, or a clean line across the sea
to a place you flew once. Think of the time
and things we accumulate, all the while growing
more conscious of losing and leaving. Aging,
our bodies collect wrinkles and scars
for each place the world would not give
under our weight. Our thoughts get laced
with strange aches, sweet as the final chord
that hangs in a guitar's blond torso.

Think how a particular ridge of hills
from a summer of your childhood grows

in significance, or one hour of light—
late afternoon, say, when thick sun flings
the shadow of Virginia creeper vines
across the wall of a tiny, white room
where a girl makes love for the first time.
Its leaves tremble like small hands
against the screen while she weeps
in the arms of her bewildered lover.
She's too young to see that as we gather
losses, we may also grow in love;
as in passion, the body shudders
and clutches what it must release.

Freight

Now I see that the first boy I loved
loved speed for its own sake the way
we all loved our bodies before learning
to feel ashamed. He built plywood ramps
on parking lots all over town and crouched
on a skateboard as it swooped and shot
across asphalt. His orange VW careened
down steep mountain roads the one night
we sneaked off and drove almost to dawn.
Yet he could be patient, sweet,
unable to believe I'd never been kissed
at fifteen, though I earnestly practiced
tilting my head back, fluttering eyelids,
tonguing the end of my fist so I'd know
what to do when he took me in his arms
in the dark in the woods when I would not
refuse what I knew must be the drive
that can wreck a girl, despite her own
intentions. That whole brutal summer
I pulled weeds in my father's garden,
my body stunned by its great momentum
and a halting restraint like bad brakes.
Once I stood up light-headed in the sun
certain I'd drop over dead with desire,
dense and pure as lead in my veins,
but I never succumbed, and in the end
we both accused the other of loving less.
For the next decade I plodded through school

and married while he dropped out, drove
customized vans to dealers throughout
the Midwest, then moved east, delivering
papers too precious to fax. Last I heard,
he works for the railroad running freight
through Pennsylvania at night when tracks
are clear of passenger trains. Sometimes
I wake to a distant whistle and think
of his engine somewhere in the mountains
rushing toward Baltimore or Williamsport,
nothing to stop him.

The Sun Lover

The long afternoon after church
a girl lies on the lawn,
glazed thighs slightly parted,
fingers splayed like petals. At sixteen
she is a virgin. While her parents nap
in the quiet house, she knows
the sun is teaching her about love,
how it comes over your body
making every muscle go soft
in its pitiless gaze,

how it penetrates everything,
changing you into something dark
and radiant. She craves it,
knows it is everywhere like God's love,
but difficult to find. She waits,
entirely still, trying to see her eyelids—
not lingering traces, but the lids themselves
luminous and red as the cheeks of the kid
who stuck a flashlight in his mouth at camp.
She squints so the tips of her lashes
flash like iridescent fish scales.

Every hour, she turns over but prefers
to face the sun. All her life
she'll measure loves against this
gentle ravishing. She'll spend afternoons
alone on crowded beaches, and at home

stand naked before mirrors, amazed
by the pale shape of her suit. She'll touch
her cheekbones' tingling pink, and nip
at her lover's shoulder, as if
it were earth she were after.

Sinning

When I was seven, Mom asked if I knew
what rabbits in the hutch were up to.
"Fucking," farm cousins told me long before.
"We call it intercourse," she said
and began the cautionary tales right then—
hurry-up weddings generations back, and look
at the children now: moved away, sloppy,
overweight. Her own name, like the state's,
a reminder forever of a virgin queen,
and her mother's name—Vesta, a pagan
goddess, but her servants were virgins.
At thirteen, I took classes to learn how to ease
my behind into couches without looking down,
to cross legs at the ankles, not knees, and keep hands
cupped on my lap. In *Becoming a Woman*, I read
a fast girl is a blighted rose, no man
wants handled merchandise. I watched sad,
young couples lean together to mumble a confession
before God and a titillated congregation,
earning the kind of church wedding where
everyone turns to check if the bride is showing.
What other sin got such attention? No wonder
I grew weary of bearing that cargo
and finally chose a boy with a saint's name
who would moan from deep in his throat,
"Oh, my God," when I finally broke.

Flu

1918, 1992

This year's flu is named for some place in Asia,
and there *is* something alien about the way
it multiplies gravity, pinning my head
to a clammy pillowcase, leaving me weak
and grasping for railings like an old woman.

Like our ancient neighbor, Bucky—
when just seventeen and halfway home
from the mill, he fell with his lunch pail.
It took two men to drag him up the hill
to his sister who nursed him all winter,

soaking bloody flecks from his handkerchiefs,
holding spoonfuls of broth to his lips
while he watched her face's reflection
shine in the bowl. By spring she was too weak
to leave bed; in less than a month

she lay dead. Sick so long, he missed his call
to ship off for Europe, that other chance to die.
Decades later, he still insists that flu was spread
by German spies scattering microbes in train depots.

He plants according to the almanac: petunias put out
in the dark of the moon grow leggy, bloom late
as I did, though he tracked my height
on a cellar door frame, a dated line for each time
he backed me against it, driving his tongue

into my mouth. The newspaper says this year's flu
has closed schools and filled hospitals;
soon even his quivering hands will be still.
Then I'll send him off in a dark, little boat

lined with all the Christmas cards he's sent
through the years, all the birthday cards,
and the stiff ten-dollar bills they contained,
blameless and clean, cash.

Ghost

In stories brought back from brief deaths,
ghosts hover above frantic doctors,
hoping they will not find a way to pull
souls back into wracked bodies.
One of those ghosts slipped out
when I was a child and a man caressed
the cleft in my panties. In all memories
I see the scene from three feet away.

Later, the ghost sat in a backseat
admiring my boyfriend's face
as it shifted in a kiss,
his hand drifting across a shoulder
to a breast. Even in marriage, the ghost
taunts from above the bed: *Is it good?*

Walking home late from the train,
I press a key between each knuckle of my fist.
(Why don't I think it would help me to scream?)
Instead the ghost foresees it all from above,
and I rage against the vulnerable socket
I cannot gouge out of this body.

To keep the ghost in place, I lift weights,
strain against that good force
binding me to earth. Mine, I instruct
my brain, my strong arms, my fists,
my sweat, the ache of myself in my calves.
And I straddle my love like a bench,
pressing hard so my thighs bulge up
into all their beautiful shapes.

I take the sun like a lover, lie naked
under its radiant gaze, finally safe,
as when a young man faces me on the train
and begins to sketch my crossed legs.
Can I take the touch of his eyes
tracing an ankle, moving up my black tights
from five feet away? *All flesh is grass.*

The priest gently lifts my bangs
and strokes a cross of ash on my forehead,
Remember, from dust you were made.
By morning, it's soot in my pores.

A Pass

Forgive us our trespasses
as we forgive, I softly recite

among strangers, remembering
the hand of an older man

gliding up my thin dress.
I twist free of him,

keep speaking as if he is just
a rich family friend chatting,

and I am still safe
in the shape of my skin.

Of course, it sets me back,
as each death resurrects

the memory of all other deaths,
and you must return to mourn

your full store of passings afresh.
A child cannot be accused

of seducing a neighbor man,
but as the girl grows, the bones

of her cheeks and pelvis jut
like blades beneath her skin,

gorgeous weapons of revenge.
At last, the lusts of *those*

who trespass against us bear
some resemblance to our own:

shame and rage, heavy as coins
sewn in the lining of an exile's coat.

When an immigrant ship went down
in Lake Erie, passengers who refused

to shed their heavy garments
drowned, yards from shore.

Bulbs

Though he was still growing, the boy ate
one meal a week during the occupation,
onion soup thickened with wallpaper paste.
His father, an expert at false walls,
hid Jews, and whatever neighbors were left
dug up tulip beds and stewed the bulbs
their ancestors had smuggled from Turks.

Nights, he dreamed pastry, cream, the white
cheeks of the starving he'd seen on the street.
The rest of his life he couldn't drink enough
coffee or work late enough to resist sleep.
He photographed lilies, torturer's tongs,
town squares where sixteenth-century martyrs
burned in the last extermination

that made any sense. He photographed
his daughter and me, twelve and fourteen,
laughing at the conservatory flower show,
then took us to tea, still giddy
with the purple-blue scent
of forced hyacinths in February.
Leaning against the tender green sleeve
of his corduroy jacket, safe

in Pittsburgh, I could not imagine
a land where skeletons don't rest long
before graves are cleared, and a dyked sea
threatens always to drown the living.
There is no pure use for history. Years later
when I hear the rumors and accusations,
I will refuse to slap his famished hand,
even when it reaches for a breast,
round and esculent as a bulb.

Onion, Fruit of Grace

Onion, fruit of grace,
you swell in the garden
hidden as the heart of God,
but you are not about religion.
Onion, frying into all those Os,
you are a perfect poet,
and you are not about that.
Onion, I love you,
you sleek, auburn beauty,
you break my heart though
I know you don't mean
to make me cry.

Peeling your paper skin,
I cry. Chopping you,
I cry. Slicing off
your wiry roots,
I cry like a penitent
at communion, onion.
Tasting grace, layer by layer,
I eat your sweet heart
that burns like the Savior's.
The sun crust you pull on
while you're still underground,

I've peeled it.
Onion, I'm eating
God's tears.

The Knowledge of Good and Evil

When beautiful Snow White bit and swooned
on the dwarfs' cottage stoop, pale bosom heaving,
and a chuckling crone scooted off with her basket
of ruby apples, I shrieked, kicking theater seats.
No hushing would stop me, so I was dragged across
strangers' knees, up a dark, inclined aisle, over
the lobby's red carpet, past ushers sharing smirks
with a candy case lady, out onto the sidewalk
which was just there on Clay Avenue in Jeannette,
Pennsylvania. The glassworks was still going
and Gillespie's still sent receipts in pneumatic tubes
when you bought a slip or new pair of shoes. Only then
I stopped screaming and grasped my shuddering breath,
blinking at parking meters, grateful it was still light
outside that story, which was worse than disobedience
or the snake I saw slithering beyond the frame
of my Bible story page. I'd studied Adam's face
and Eve, who tempted him, hair hiding her breasts
as they walked in that exotic garden, already bent
over with guilt, palm fronds at their waists.
Mom coaxed me back to the lobby, and I hovered
in buttery light by the popcorn machine. *The prince
returns! She comes back to life! Go in and see!*
she crooned with the ushers, but I refused. Even when
they pushed me toward a crack in the dark double doors
and I glimpsed a prince and lavish wedding dress,
I could not believe she was alive and happy ever after.
I was a heretic too insulted by the cross

to accept resurrection. I knew that marriage
is just a trick cooked up by the grownups
to keep me from screaming my head off.

Eve's Striptease

Lingerie shopping with Mom, I braced myself
for the wedding night advice. Would I seem
curious enough, sufficiently afraid? Yet
when we sat together on their bed, her words
were surprisingly wise:
>   Whatever happens, remember this—
>   it keeps getting better and better.
She had to be telling the truth. At ten,
I found a jar of Vaseline in her nightstand,
its creamy grease gouged deep, and dusting
their room each week, I marked the decline
of bedside candles. But she didn't say lust
is a bird of prey or tell me the passion
she passed on to me is no protector of borders.
She'd warned me only about the urges men get
and how to save myself from them. Though
she'd flirt with any greenhouse man
for the best cabbage flats, any grease monkey
under the hood, she never kissed anyone but Dad.
How could she guess that with *Jesus Loves Me*
on my tongue, constantly suffering crushes
on uncles, I would come to find that
almost everything gets better and better?
The tiny bird she set loving in me must
keep on, batting the bars of its cage
in a rage only matched by my cravings
for an ample pantry and golden anniversary.
She let me learn for myself all the desires

a body can hold, how they grow stronger
and wilder with age, tugging in every direction
until it feels my sternum might split
like Adam's when Eve stepped out,
sloughing off ribs.

Mother Love

My mother hoards baby dresses.
She never speaks of them, but I know
starched frocks collect in a bottom drawer,
bought from consignment shops on her way
to some other errand, their smocked yokes
embroidered with tiny roses too gorgeous
to pass up. I know she pities me,
each year growing more accomplished
as my eggs wait in their dark carton,
marked with dates for release
and expiration. Pregnant friends
who once devoted their bodies to sex
and professional suits are vigilant:
no tap water, no bottom-feeding fish,
no coffee, not one drop of wine.
Ancient Hebrew texts used the same word
to name Adam's toil and Eve's labor
pains: humanity's curse is work
toward no certain end, the anguish of love
and not knowing. Mom bites her tongue,
politely inquires after my job, then
complains that people still ask her why
I remain childless. I know she can't explain
how her only daughter could be so smart
and not see that even I would not exist
if she and my father had waited until
they could afford it or knew for sure
that their marriage would hold. Time

passes, she grows heavy and soft with all
we can't say, longing to give her love
to a girl guileless and simple enough
to take it without question or doubt.

The Secrets of Marriage

Dinner parties are never as much
for the guests as for after
when we stand in porch light,
his arm across my shoulder.
Good night, Thanks for coming,
Watch your step. And I'm back
in the kitchen where Mom's face reflects
in a dark window, and Dad drifts
from table to sink, handing her plates.
He lifts fat from the roaster,
scrapes broth and limp onions
into a bowl. *Is there a lid*
for this hon? Barely discernible
from my room, their murmurs
concern the guests—*Did you hear him say,*
What did she mean by—talk trailing off
in a soft clatter of flatware.
By breakfast, china was stacked
in the cupboard, hand-washed goblets
were lined up behind glass. What moved
between them those nights was
as mysterious as algebra, the first
subject that confounded me to tears.
Effort counted for nothing when
I struggled at the blackboard,
and a stupid mistake in subtraction
wrecked the whole equation
in front of everyone. The secrets

of marriage seemed to be theorems
learned and followed on faith:
invert and multiply, what you do
to the left, you must do
to the right to take away desire
or pain. What you want is to arrive
at an improbable compromise,
your elegant calculation
tapering down the page
to render the true
value of X.

Storm

See the woman pulled from bed by a storm
blowing in off the prairie, wind-drawn,
scarcely aware that she's out on the porch
in only her nightshirt. Now see the man
in boxers who finds her. Their startled eyes
show they both know what can happen when
wind thrashes the elms and stains the sky.
Now feel that moment grow solid as a bone
china cup, luminous when held up to light
before it's put back in the cupboard. That
breath before words so laden they might,
one day in memory, finally collapse
against the other's stunned form instead
of mumbling something and returning to bed.

Word to Measure Space

Away from you, the ninth-grade word returns:
Planaria, those blunt-headed worms
that cling to stones pulled up from mud.
I flicked some into jars and fed them blood
from liver bits until the day in school
when we learned how they reproduce when cut.
At my desk, I squirmed as the teacher slit
the tip of a tail. Halves writhed side by side
like lovers, till they wrenched their head apart.
Only a twitch for a brain, yet that pain
I felt was when we part and there persist
the same dark slits upon our hearts,
as dumb as worms to name their loss
and with no mind to measure space.

Definition: To Fix

A matchbook slipped under a table leg.
The lover's face sharpening in a tray

of darkroom brine. The way humming
is rolled into notes and strung on a staff

or how telling your life to a shrink
becomes your life, each memory a prophecy.

Does confessing something make it a sin
or only convert shame into a keepsake,

beloved because it survived oblivion?
The heart that cannot forget its desire

drags the body behind it like a driver
who, admiring a lily along the road,

ends up in the ditch. Or that orange lily,
if only she knew the force of her allure,

how petals peeled back and spread by the sun
resemble the sun. In fractal geometry

a molecule of sand from a Finnish beach
can map the whole Scandinavian coast.

How to measure what drives a car north,
late, on a fine night for fishing except

by time or the numbers of license and interstate;
how to tell whether the cat fattening on a sill

can recall clawing her way across
the living room rug, howling like a baby.

Sixth Anniversary

What separates us from the cats
yowling like famished newborns
behind our old house is that
we can choose how we'll act,
though there's no controlling
how the bump of a near-stranger's
elbow could light up my back
in a room of dull cocktail chatter.
Six years into this marriage,
I admit that some summer nights
I long for an air conditioner—
anything to drown out those cats—
I am that jealous of their
groaning under our window,
which seems to be the voice
of that old, insufferable itch
we scratched until we were raw,
then emerged, groggy, to prowl
the streets for dinner,
a smarting between our legs.

By now, my body must feel as familiar
as the gold hills outside Fresno
scattered with tufts of scrub oak,
where for hours each day you rode
a racing bike, its light frame
fused with your own. You knew
each hole and bump in the road,
each place your weight shifted,

and pedaling up into the Sierra
you once lifted above your body,
hung there, watching your thighs
pump with each rasp of breath,
as sometimes making love, I see us,
gripped by our slow heaving,
and wonder what form of animal
we finally are, who crave
both safety and hunger.

The New Place

We can't admit that we can't make love
in our old bed positioned like this.
You no longer cook, and I seem to know

only three recipes. The towel racks
on the floor hoard lint, and like drunks
who can't see past a need to stay numb

we sit in our rooms unable to work.
You spend long days in the city and return
to me, talking, but silence always

catches up. You think the place is possessed,
and I blame the broom we moved despite
that superstition against dragging old

dirt into new rooms. I can't even pitch
scorched pot holders or properly mourn
those turquoise walls, dull with eight years

of our own grease and happiness. Maybe we grew
so fond of the known that we can't arrange
ourselves here, and we'll just have to chuck

something out with the oversized bookcase
and table, or else take a saw to it all
and see what turns up with the dust.

Wife of a Resident Alien

I thought it was just a matter of recipes
or learning his non-English words.

How could I guess he'd get obsessed
with records cut before he was born,

that our dinners would be accompanied
by tunes his parents would have hummed

if they'd been sipping cocktails
in California when they were young,

instead of getting by in British Columbia
and Brazil? I thought washing the trousers

he brings home from thrift shops
could finally fade their mute histories,

the shapes of strangers' legs draining
with the suds. I may have even believed

my grandmother's quilts and plates could
compensate for a whole transient century,

that if he told me everything, each day
would connect to the last, and I'd knit

a seamless stocking stretching back
to him, a toddler on his father's arm

balanced against a deck railing
as they watch the ship's captain shove

a boxed suicide overboard, its hull pointed
toward North America. As if loving him

like this, I could keep him from clinging
to edges the rest of his life.

Lesson of Hard-Shelled Creatures

We stopped the car on the back roads
in Mississippi and ran for turtles,
hurled them, huge and heavy
as turkey platters, into ditches,

hoping they'd have sense to stay put.
We swerved for armadillos in Texas
so their stumpy legs would make it
to safety. The shards of those creatures,

like shattered skulls on the road,
spooked us more than any soft-bodied
fox or dog in the ditch, stinking reminders
of the instant it takes to swerve

and crack up, the way a sentence can dash
domestic accord, plunging you down that slope
where words are rocks in avalanche. After,
it can take days of courtesy and careful

cooking to restore solid ground between you.
My father-in-law sent armadillo shell
earrings from Brazil with a note saying
they were glad to eat those creatures

back then, this gift like the refugee ragout
he ladles onto our plates reminds us
his mother once cooked a robin in soup,
the thin broth gritty with worms.

He can't help but decant those stories,
in case we still don't know that *anything*
can happen, and in the end we'll be glad
to eat what we find with whomever is left.

Living Large

In our next new house I crave asparagus,
pare tender shoots, arrange them in a skillet,
turn up the heat and, after ten years
of cooking for two, walk out the back door.
I admire the Japanese maple, pull a few weeds,
finger daylily buds, then race back
to the reeking kitchen, yank the pan
from its furious coil onto the Formica
which hisses a blister, then scorch
the cutting board. I say I don't know how
I can be so destructive, though I secretly
like the way those ruined shoots droop
their olive heads against charred black.
Only later I think to blame it on desire
and the road between Cody and Yellowstone,
how July snow blew across our windshield
as we searched for a site that took tenters
in spite of bears. A man from Queens,
thrilled to see New York plates, invited us
to his fire that night. They were heading West,
not sure where yet, but the wife and he
could no longer live large anywhere back East,
not even upstate. But here, he waved at a ridge
behind our heads, elk graze. When dawn broke
on that ridge, large was the taste of coffee
I sipped in the sun by a patch of sage
until the love of my youth touched my neck,
saying come, meaning back to the tent,

pointed true east and lit like a lantern.
We knew to lock food and utensils in the trunk,
that bears will maul a menstruating woman,
and a sow and cubs were feeding on a carcass
not distant. Nonetheless we filled our tent
with good human scent, missing a chance
to wish the couple from Queens a safe trip.

Before Dawn in October

The window frame catches a draft
that smells of dead leaves and wet street,
and I wrap arms around my knees,
look down on these small breasts,
so my spine forms a curve as perfect
as the rim of the moon. I want to tell
the man sleeping curled as a child beside me
that this futon is a raft. The moon
and tiny star we call sun are the parents
who at last approve of us. For once,
we haven't borrowed more than we can return.
Stars above our cement backyard are as sharp
as those that shine far from Brooklyn,
and we are not bound for anything worse
than we can imagine, as long as we turn
on the kitchen lamp and light a flame
under the pot, as long as we sip coffee
from beautiful China-blue cups and love
the steam of the shower and thrusting
our feet into trousers. As long as we walk
down our street in sun that ignites
red leaves on the maple, we will see
faces on the subway and know we may take
our places somewhere among them.

Our Last Neighborhood
in Brooklyn

They said the only way to fit in
is get pregnant or talk Italian.
Failing both, it took me a year and a half
to realize the brown-robed men in gardens
are not Josephs to accompany all the Marys
but Saint Anthony of Padua, patron
of barren women and all things lost
except causes, which are the purview
of Jude. Lily stalk in one arm, the child
I mistook for Our Savior in the other,
Anthony met Francis himself in Sicily
which explains why he fits so well here
among plum tomato vines and fig trees
that old men prune and wrap in cotton batting
each fall like armless Venuses bound
for museums. As long as they're faithful,
these trees will keep putting out
exotic leaves, plumping their sweet fruits
in the sun which darkens the faces and arms
of longshoremen and garbage men and men
of no certain vocation who sit in T-shirts
on kitchen chairs outside social clubs
on Court Street. If you have to sell fast,
bury Saint Joseph upside down in the back
garden, they told us, then gave us one.
Just in case, I forced his porcelain
shoulders into the fine dirt between hostas
and faded impatiens. It's safe,
they said, a good neighborhood, meaning

you can turn a corner of shaded brownstones
and see your husband of many years walking
toward you. His face will seem younger,
a smile breaking so easily it will nearly erase
all the effort it has taken to keep a household
between you. The neighbors decorate with music
and light the whole dim season, Halloween to Easter,
but chiefly at Christmas, when a virgin
who never stopped being a virgin—
even after bearing other children—
gave birth, her miraculous gift enacted
each time the subway crowns the tunnel
at Carroll to climb the Culver overpass
between Mary Star of the Sea Convent
and the greasy waters of the Gowanus Canal,
which was the first piece of Brooklyn
the Indians lost to the Dutch.

Loud

When a woman who grew up in Flatbush
moved to New Jersey, she tore up
the garden there, refusing to grow anything
from the old neighborhood, no Red Emperor
tulips in May, no geraniums loud
as fire trucks, no hydrangeas. No,
especially not those cartoon shrubs
that hog up whole corners of Brooklyn lawn,
blooming hot pink or cerulean, ecstatic
as Hispanic baby showers. It was all too much—

whatever reminded her of Ablemarle Road
where rose of Sharon trees gush
lavender and pink across back alleys,
shameless, where each June saints' grottoes
are overcome with heavy, red ramblers
planted to remind us of the rosary,
and portulacas squeeze magenta
in sidewalk cracks. People who planted
this borough must have had some kind of hunger
only color could feed, like the new citizens
you see on the street, clashing bright
plaid shirts against striped pants.

Children, reaching for the reddest crayon,
when do we learn what is too much?
When do we start averting our eyes
at overdone Puerto Rican girls on the train,
taking it all in anyway: lush fuchsia

43

lips and nails, black hair heaped
into confections? When do we start
calling flowers and women "cheap,"
as if life were a sale? Are we so far gone
we don't know how to praise them, loud
as the shopkeepers on Church Avenue
who save insults for their best customers?
Carmine, the butcher who loves me, shouts
Wadda ya want with chicken breasts?
Don't you know white meat makes you ugly?

On Leaving Brooklyn

after Psalm 137

If I forget thee
let my tongue forget the songs
it sang in this strange land
and my heart forget the secrets
only a stranger can learn.

Borough of churches, borough of crack,
if I forget how ailanthus trees sprout
on the rooftops, how these streets
end in water and light,
let my eyes grow nearsighted.

Let my blood forget
the map of its travels
and my other blood cease
its slow tug toward the sea
if I do not remember,

if I do not always consider thee
my Babylon, my Jerusalem.

45

II MAP OF THE KNOWN WORLD

The Use of Allusion

States away from where I grew up, this prairie
smells like home tonight: goldenrod on the edge
of bloom. Wild rose hips, green when I arrived,
are bloody bulbs. This is one way to mark time.

In the Tang Dynasty's last days, Li Shang-Yin wrote
"wax teardrops," leaving readers forever to guess
all that transpired while the candle burned,
all that could make a concubine cry.

I'm beginning to understand the use of allusion:
how one scent or gesture can stand for
all absent others. In these clear eyes, for instance,
I can almost peer through to all the eyes

I've loved since mother. Aligned like this,
each one grows more precious in a complex
lineage of attachment and loss, gathering weight
in the body, even as it shrinks toward death.

Yes, love collects in us like trace heavy metals,
all that was left when tooth and bone vaporized
at Hiroshima. You can still see those dim
human shadows blasted against a granite wall.

Map of the Known World

When Mom called me to the tub I'd kneel
and drape hot cloths like bandages
across the scar that will always be
two years older than me. She'd moan
as I scrubbed its topography,
skin grafts still itching years after
the doctor patched her shoulder
with tissue lifted from thighs.
When a surgeon peeled scalded skin
from my leg, it came from exactly that spot,
a kitchen injury like women get.

For two weeks I lay, ate beef,
couldn't bear the touch of even
a bed sheet. Each day I'd spread salve
like frosting and try to grasp reasons
the way true believers eke meaning
from every disaster. In the end,
I learned the mind can't hold pain,
only facts:
       She was in the burn ward so long,
       her child forgot who she was.
       She worked rope through a pulley
       to teach her arm to lift again.

And because she rolled on the floor,
I could be born to love the one
layer of tissue out of seven that survived,
astounding me each time I'd unwind gauze
to find the true, moral nature of skin
which just returns, brilliant and pink—
a map of the known world in ancient times,
shaped ragged by exploration and fear,
spread across my thigh.

July 1969

Mom's driving the Impala through Delaware
where land relaxes toward the shore
and the roadside is lined with black men
selling tomatoes and sweet cantaloupes.
My brother's up front reading the map,
the baby we left at an uncle's, and Dad
is in San Francisco all week on business.
He doesn't know our mother withdrew
one hundred bucks and packed the trunk.
I am about to start second grade.
She is almost the age of Jesus and about
to slide into a terrible depression,
but not yet. The back of her neck is so serene
she must know this week we will be happy
to eat pizza and twenty-nine-cent burgers.
We'll adore her striding toward us, the sea
glistening on her black, shirred suit.
Sun will sling low over the roller coaster
when we reach the porch of our boardinghouse
with its turrets and worn rose carpets,
its elaborate rules about which stairs
to use if you're dressed for the beach.
The starched sheets and pillow slips
will scrape shoulders and cheekbones
still stinging with Noxema when I climb
into bed beside her. About that time,
Dad will be slicing into a rare steak
somewhere on the other coast, and back home
beans will be getting hard in the garden.

Ladies' Night at the Turkish
and Russian Baths

Outside, it's any tenement on East Tenth Street;
at the head of the stairs I drop my watch,
keys, wallet into a slender metal box
and take a robe of thin cotton sheeting.
Past the case of smoked fish, I pull off
my clothes among napping strangers and descend
marble steps stained with a century's grit.

In the steam room, an old woman looks up;
slender gourds hang off the cage of her ribs,
and when she wrings the pink cloth on her crotch,
I see a bun, bald as a girl's, and think *crone*,
ashamed. She runs weary eyes down my form,
then closes them.

Along the plunge pool, supple women stroke
green mud on their cheekbones and stretch
their legs between plastic palms. Above them,
a compote of brilliant tile fruit and the name
of an Italian mason. I love to think of him
telling his son about this place, or how it was
in the thirties, filled with immigrants
from cold-water flats, one of them
with eyes like Franz Kafka could not afford
to come here, but did, breathing steam for hours,
not needing to remember the names of things,
only sweating out the soot of New York, safe

as I feel in the hot cave where women drape
between streaming spigots. Some murmur,
most are silent, except when one
grabs a bucket and dumps it onto her chest
with a groan. Our eyes meet and we grin,
grateful to show and view the real shapes
of ourselves: so many different breasts
and hips that get smoothed over by clothes,
none of us looking like we're supposed to!

And after, our hair wrapped up in towels,
we climb to a roof that faces the back
of Ninth Street where strangers pass by lit
windows, cooking dinner, opening letters.
We stretch out there on cots, and beside me
tears slide like sweat into the turban
of a stunning young woman. Whatever
the reason, I feel bound to her weeping,
eyes locked on our city's sky
aglow with all that lies beneath it.

Coat of a Visiting Nurse

I put on Mom's coat the way we put on
the clothes of the dead, out of duty
or thrift or because I could not refuse.
Machine wash, she urged, permanent press,
this zip-out lining will take you
into November most years.

Walking alone in it, I think of the way
we remember those who've gone on,
frozen in one frame of their lives,
slightly heroic: she drives a tiny VW
on an unmarked country road toward
a trailer where a man is dying,
his wife worn out by his yellowing form
on the couch. His cancer, neatly charted
on Mom's clipboard. A stern jaw,
sturdy shoes, and this practical coat
are her only defenses against death
or a flat tire in wet weather.

As sleek city ladies stride past me
on the street, this stiff oatmeal coat,
which she grew too stout
to button and had to pass on,
feels conspicuous, indestructible
as so much I stand to inherit.

Lymphoma

Perhaps I should call your disease by its name
and admit that pain has no meaning, nothing to redeem it,

but I was gripped by beauty again this morning,
peeling the shell off a hard-boiled egg;

outside, the hydrangeas were heaps of light
on the lawn, harsh and brilliant. (Your skin

is now that pale.) And in the meadow
cabbage butterflies lifted like flakes

of lead white paint above white crests
of Queen Anne's lace in light so pure,

I ached. The lit stove: that vital blue exists
in the intricate veins of your wrist

and the map I now see on your scalp.
Clearly as a child, you sketch death—

the back of a rabbi walking fluorescent wards,
his long, black coat and *pais* blowing out—

and the delivery from death—yourself the Pietà
in a blue hospital gown. Claiming no formal faith,

you draw out these meanings as I cling to words,
binding whatever I know to what I do not,

calling it all other names: your lymph nodes,
for instance, are new potatoes lodged against

a loaf of lung. Anything to comfort,
to tame. How can I think we have not found

meaning in this—or faith in the way we clutch
each other, each time I arrive or leave?

Flammable Skirts Recalled

Have you seen the photo of an Indian skirt ablaze
on a mannikin's legs? The newspaper recalled
a quarter million of the ones we bought that night
at Marshall's, love-struck as my great aunts
who used to sew identical dresses. In the parking lot
you asked if I thought all the sadness of our twenties
might have been grief in advance. Maybe time isn't
continuous, and there are pains too great to be held
by the present. So when we met over a decade ago,
you already carried a child with my name, whose heart
would need mending with bits of other live hearts.
When she was born, I learned it's bad luck for Jews
to name babies for the living, as if recalling
the names of the dead could keep history's thread
pulling smoothly from its spool. I didn't ask bad luck
for whom; that spring I won prizes while she was in surgery.
One night on a train, I misread an acupuncture ad
promising cures for insomnia, backache, *heartache*
—no, *headache:* small Julia, namesake not-namesake,
sharp pin in a mother's heart. Should we return
these skirts or keep wearing them, Ellen, knowing
any instant the sheer turquoise paisley could catch
a flicked ash and ignite? Haven't we—like at least
a quarter million others—always been living like this?

Answer

I am the one who dives into a pool
and comes up from that turquoise
clutching her head in the sunlight.
I am the one the nurses must wake
all night long asking, "What is today?"
"What is sixteen divided by eight?"
If answering keeps me from slipping
away, I'll be the one they send home
in the morning, a woolly ache murmuring
concussion, concussion against my brain,
afraid for life of diving and unable
to shake the powdery scent of the nurse
who insisted, "Tell us your name,
please say who you are!"

Why I Ran

You can't predict what you'll do
at dusk when two thugs circle in

on you and a friend at the end of a pier,
how you'll move when they block

your escape, threatening a gun
in their jackets. You only know after,

and then there's no telling why, for instance,
I ran. Though I believe what they say—

you can lose your life trying to save it—
this just comes down to the dumb sense of legs,

as when, not yet seven, my cousin and I
saw a bull charging across the pasture

and, without word or second glance, ran
until we tore through the fence, panting,

stunned by a red scrap of my dress
caught in the barbed wire's knot.

On that pier, I looked back to see
my friend talking his way through a robbery

rational as any transaction, but because
he had no cash, they came for me.

I took their shoves at first, stupidly
refusing to give up seven bucks.

Blame it on that old bull or the difference
between those who grow up in pastures

and those who come from suburban homes,
but later that friend confessed

one fleeting thought: he almost leapt
into the Hudson's shimmering net.

How It Looks from South Brooklyn

Rocco's pigeons circle in shoals like fish
above Clinton Street, bank and drift in thin
April light that glints off their wings.

Do they ever collide or fly away
when he whistles them back to their rooftop
cages? Has he ever watched one, released

from his car trunk along some grassy roadside
upstate, drop like a rock from the sky?
Not for me I'm asking, this week before Easter

when you'd think belief in the resurrection
of the body ought to come easy. When soul
won't stir, it sits, dense as the wooden thumb

at the center of a Russian doll, just
a small, dumb version of herself,
eyes shrunken to paint dots.

Where does Rocco get rid of bird shit
in Brooklyn, where earth is sealed up tight
with cement? Someone I almost know lies dead

as the stone they rolled from the tomb,
but still living. Does it take more faith
to mourn a loss or expect miracles?

Every window in this apartment has bars,
and the door has a lock for each day
the Savior lay in the grave,

as though it's that easy to know
what we're supposed to keep out
and what we should try to keep in.

To Honor the Dead

> Who is this God who refuses,
> What does the book of life want to tell us.
>
> ALICIA SUSKIN OSTRIKER

Let not his soul be judged
by the God of my fathers, who is frugal,
hard-working, faithful, and true,
or let his soul be judged by that old Hebrew
God who couldn't help falling over Himself
in love with adulterous David, and who
disclosed little about the hereafter,
choosing instead to bless those who give
it all away now. Even the rabbi wept
admonishing us not to project his soul
into the heavens, but instead to erect
our memories here, like the homeless men
on Amsterdam Avenue who still miss him.
*There are too many no's in the world
to add one more,* he'd say, then stop,
talk with them, dig in his pocket
for change, as if he hadn't said this
the last time it took twenty minutes
to walk two blocks for coffee.
When young women nobody knew showed up
sobbing at the funeral, we just assumed
that was more of his shtick—
how he'd reminisce about a graceful age
between the Pill and naming of AIDS.
No one under thirty believed him.

When he was a kid in Bensonhurst,
the world was only Italians and Jews.
Italians beat their wives, his mother said,
Jews cheat, better a lover than a brute.
Where I came from, only kids got hit,
and we grew up too obedient to speak
of adultery, yet I loved him that instant
on Sixth Avenue after he'd paid for a dinner
I couldn't afford, and a sudden gust rent
his coat as he told how a surgeon slit
from neck to naval, splitting his ribs
so his heart lay beating and guileless
as a fetus. *Like a chicken!*
he wept, clutching his chest, stalled
on the sidewalk. *They kill you almost,*
then he grinned as he must have grinned
on the gurney rushing toward surgery,
handing a wad of cash to his wife,
grandiose as Jesus commanding ,
If anything terrible happens, buy supper
for everyone in the waiting room!

Houseguest Confession

I woke with the urge to creep
from my room, sneak up behind you
writing a sermon in your precise script
at the dining room table, and throw
my arms around your neck, which I did.
The earth did not slip from its spot
in the universe. Nothing we said about God
the night before, sinking deeper
into our cups, offending each other
and the heavens, got unsaid.
Your Oma, coaxed by Opa to let
her crimped hair hang loose
for the photograph, still lost
her grass gardens and fine pleated dress.
All of old Russia remained lost.
Your *Kröger* clock stayed silent behind
its flat roses. The blue onion plates
bought in homage to prewar bourgeois taste
survived your divorce, but East Germany,
where they were made, must have collapsed as did
your father, whose overstuffed sofas cramp
the apartment. Lost, too, are moments caught
in snapshots you tape to bookcases and door frames.
Truth is, that fine Saturday morning
New Yorkers all over the city continued
to lose jobs, lose their faith,
lose homes and mates. By what else
do we measure life's progress? I guess

my reckless gesture restored nothing,
but for a moment I could hold
the shape of your shoulders and press
this reminder into your chest:
you of all things are not lost
on East Nineteenth Street in this
glorious patch of sunlight; whatever
you are, whoever you will become,
you are embraced this instant
at your table's blazing white linen.

Brooklyn Bridge Showing Painters
on Suspenders, 1914

after an anonymous photograph from the
Municipal Archives of the City of New York

I love how these men, defying the gut's
inexorable wedge, lounge like millionaires
on suspension cables above the East River.
Lines catch two of them in the small of the back,
jutting their brutal hips forward. One
in a bowler and bright jacket buttons
leans casually as against a porch post;
another sits as if on a sofa, his foot hooked
to safety. Their indiscernible faces are cocky,
as working-class handsome as the firemen
with foreheads like spades who swaggered
into our apartment to check gas burners
after a water main break. All ten painters
are past danger now, buried in huge cemeteries
in Brooklyn or Queens, miniature cities
where polished headstones flash sunlight
at passing trains. Dead, too, the photographer
who set them forever in a question mark
across this steel web, just twenty years
before you were born.

When did you begin to imagine bridges
like the one we crossed last month
headed toward sun and Manhattan's shore
obscured here by intermittent steam bursts?
When did you start to imagine death?
Born the year your first book enraged
a Mennonite village, I am half your age
and ripe for a child but have none,
so I love relentlessly whatever connects
my life to the rest. Remember the night
you clutched my hand on East Tenth Street
as if breath were lodged there? I held on
hard until we turned the corner at Third Avenue
where Tony was killed four Octobers ago.
Momentarily touching that metal phone stall
I prayed *light perpetual shine upon us,*
knowing we dare not let go of even sorrow,
that hanging on, fearless and afraid
as these men, is our only home.

The Streak

A boy hammers a piece of lead pipe
against the lip of a watering trough
until it is thin and flat as a coin
then cuts it into slender strips
his sister will pinch on her snake-black
braids. In this, the boy learns
even heavy, hard things can be beaten
into other things, transformed entirely,
the way milkweed's translucent parachutes
become the stuffing for a soldier's coat.
Collecting the pods along a field lane,
the boy hums, thinking of a man in his coat
drifting under a white, silk scallop
somewhere above Europe, cold up there,
silent, so far from any place where
farmers must save even corn husks
to stuff their children's mattress ticks.
How his mattress rustles each time he shifts,
dreaming, the way dry cornfields scuff
in the wind. One day this boy will turn
from sleep to rouse a woman, then
turn back, the streak on her thigh,
a slug's bright leaving, and I,
his only daughter, will come of that.

Migraines, for Dad

About these we will always agree:

how they sneak up unexpectedly
to streak our eyes with silvery stars

how tingling numbs our fingers and arms
and our tongues lie limp and thick

and cannot form words. We speak
as though some spiritual gift

shrinks our skulls so uselessly thin
they shelter our brains against nothing

as though we are exceptionally brave
walking around with heads that ache

in the sunlight. Yet with each return
from the pain, we're articulate,

feline, and once more alone.

Learning the Names

Sunday afternoons we learned to love nature
by naming it. On the path behind Dad
I'd answer sassafras, thrusting a fist
of evidence: one leaf like a mitten, one
like a fish, one like a pitchfork, all grown
from one tree, like two brothers and me.
Like Aquinas, I learned to carry the names
of whatever God made in my head. To never
think tree, but hemlock or shag-bark
hickory, even the next spring
to remember yolk yellow leaves
and nut hulls we smashed between rocks
to eat their sweet, milky meats.
I learned this is how you use language
to know what you will never possess.
Late in March, bound in boots and scarves,
we'd compete to read the signs of spring:
maroon skunk cabbage spathes,
May apple shoots, an acorn split
by one scarlet root. And, when Dad stretched
onto a patch of crows foot and released
his long, heavy breath, I'd lie beside
that incomprehensible grown-up exhaustion
and trace an old jack pine with my eyes:
trunk, branch, twig, needles, and a tight,
green cone that would open and drop.
I knew that when we stood up, it would look
as though deer had slept there.

How My Father Learned English

Breathing his own breath,
forehead pressed in a corner
while the teacher's syllables
pelted his back, meaningless.
At some point, he says, it just
began to make sense, sounds gave
up significance as neatly
as the clear and yolk slipped
into batter when his mother tapped
a bowl and pulled eggshells apart.
How could she bear to think
of her first-grader, mute and confused
the long season from Labor Day
to Christmas, begging translation
from deskmates, pestering hired men
for names of things during chores?
She knew he'd eventually piece together
a tongue with words from home
and school. Only this fall I think
to ask how that happened, though
I've taught English for years,
eagerly asking the foreigners
to tell me about their homes,
Please, I urge, say it in English.

Letter to Timothy Russell from Lewisburg

You'd never know this place with its leaves on—
it can't compare with November or Weirton where
nothing gets this green, no sky stays this clear.
It's so idyllic, sometimes I can't stand it. Today
out of nowhere I laughed in the face of a class
and couldn't stop gasping. What could I tell them?
Our private pursuits of truth and beauty have just
been upstaged by some leaves on an ornamental cherry
that turned yellow and peach and drop, even as I speak,
onto the black walk! Of course I couldn't.
I don't know what you do in the mills, but at least
you're still forging lines to keep yourself sane.
I just talk. And I finally got my diploma,
which makes me more likely to teach than to study,
come fall, though I feel as half-baked as the leaves,
falling too early and all out of season. Please tell
how you do it: keep both your self and your job
without bursting from laughter or crashing
right out through the glass.

Black Dress

Poised as a cruise ship, Maxine Kumin
passes through the crowd, willowy and gray,
someone's grandma by now but still lovely,
and my mind goes straight to Anne Sexton—
sex pot in a coffin. Kumin says
they shared one reading outfit
down to the shoes. I see pointed pumps,
smoky hose, and a sleeveless cocktail
sheath shuttling between them,
long phone calls between suburban kitchens
to arrange who'd pick it up
at the cleaners, who needed it next,
who needed it most, as if success
could be shared that simply,
both of them knockouts at the podium
and so often confused that Sexton joked,
"They can't tell the kook from the Jew!"

I need to believe they shared
their readers' desire as easily
as they shared their ambitions—
how they read each new line
to the other breath on the Princess phone.
Or despair, how they shared babies
and breakdowns as all our slim mothers
did, stiff smiles and shifts captured
in photographs, their bare arms like fish
tangled across a dress's dark platter.
I need to know how Kumin finally survived

her own beauty to keep writing alone,
and finally stand here before me in defiance
of anyone who'd concoct a cautionary tale
of her life.

Eve's Curse

To the beautiful student, as her blue eyes glaze
and brighten in their brine, I cannot say,
Yes, it will be as you suspect. This work
will drive you away from us; it will make
you strange in the end. Though you were raised
in Pennsylvania, the state which retains
more of its natives than any other,
the only state that contains all the letters
you need to write "live," you will leave.
Because these sweet limestone fields sustained
you and all of us before this, your curse
will be to ache as you've never imagined:
your limbs will long for the scent of this ridge
as Eve's curse was to crave for her husband.

Thinking of Certain Mennonite Women

When I think I can't bear to trace
one more sorrow back to its source,

I think of Lois those summer evenings,
when, supper dishes done, she'd climb

a windmill and cling beneath its great blades,
drawing water from under her father's fields.

She'd stay there until the sun went down
on barn roof, garden, and the one paved road

pointing toward town. When I am afraid
to set out once more alone, I see Julie

pumping her legs so hard she believes
she will fly off the swing set and land

gently on the lawn. I see her let go,
braids streaking behind, then see her knees

shredded on gravel, stuck to stockings
each time she kneels to pray at a pew.

When I can't tell my own desire
from the wishes of others, I remember

my mom, too young to know or care better,
flinging her jumper, blouse, socks, and slip

into the wind, dancing for flower beds
until her mother discovers. When I wonder

how I should live this only one life,
I think of how they tell these stories:

honestly, without explanation,
to whomever will listen.

Boustrophedon

An ancient mode of writing in which lines run alternately from right
to left and from left to right. Greek: as the ox turns (in plowing).

A little boy walks behind the plow
picking up stones in a field.
He drops them onto a pile
at the end of the row.
One day these stones will make
a home for his soul. He doesn't know

this yet. How can he know
the meaning of all that the plow
inscribes: that he'll grow to make
a life from this field,
that its meanings will pile
like paint, which he'll stroke in rows,

each dab a seed in a furrow?
He'll have to leave to finally know
all that's concealed in this pile
of limestones. Rocks struck open by the plow
reveal the spiral fossils of the field.
Maybe whatever anyone can make

of himself was already made
long ago, order and disorder set in the rows
of a double helix. Settlers clearing fields
often spared single oaks, though they knew
whoever followed would have to plow
around them. Saved from the woodpile,

the trees grow elegant alone and drop piles
of acorns into the troughs that furrows make.
Some sprout, but the certain plow
turns saplings under as it carves rows
for corn. In winter, stubble slants in snow
like runes scrawled across the field.

A farmer's son who takes canvas for his field
aches to become an artist, compiles
another family, moves to a city. No
one back home sees or knows what he makes:
the way light shifts on those scarred rows
of pigment, though he paints as they plow.

It only takes one person plowing a row
to make a field, then others can follow
knowing they aren't the first or alone.

First Bird

The first bird that sings
sings for all birds, even

when she stands for nothing
but herself, a dun-colored finch

on a dogwood branch.
No telling what a bird knows,

if this seems the first time
light glowed on the horizon,

or if she thinks her beak
alone has pierced the night.

We know nothing can be whole
that hasn't been torn.

There is no holy thing
that hasn't been betrayed,

the way notes, once forced
into her tiny throat,

come out this dawn as song.

Flying Lesson

Over a tray of spent plates, I confessed
to the college president my plans to go East,
to New York, which I'd not really seen,
though it seemed the right place
for a sophomore as sullen and restless
as I had become on that merciless
Midwestern plain. He slowly stroked
a thick cup and described the nights
when, a theology teacher in Boston, he'd fly
a tiny plane alone out over the ocean,
each time pressing farther into the dark
until the last moment, when he'd turn
toward the coast's bright spine, how he loved
the way the city glittered beneath him
as he glided gracefully toward it,
engine gasping, fuel needle dead on empty,
the way sweat dampened the back of his neck
when he climbed from the cockpit, giddy.
Buttoned up in my cardigan, young, willing
to lose everything, how could I see generosity
or warning? But now that I'm out here,
his advice comes so clear: fling yourself
farther, and a bit farther each time,
but darling, don't drop.

Acknowledgments

These poems, some in different form, appeared in the following periodicals: *Artful Dodge* ("Black Dress," "Learning the Names," and "The Streak"); *Broadside* ("First Bird," "Houseguest Confession," and "The Sun Lover"); *Brooklyn Woman* ("Why I Ran"); *Cincinnati Poetry Review* ("Ladies' Night at the Turkish and Russian Bath"); *College English* ("Boustrophedon," "Flammable Skirts Recalled," and "Flu"); *Indiana Review* ("Brooklyn Bridge Showing Painters on Suspenders, 1914" and "Lesson of Hard-Shelled Creatures"); *Mennonite Life* ("Our Last Neighborhood in Brooklyn"); *Poet Lore* ("Coat of a Visiting Nurse" and "Lymphoma); *Poetry* ("First Gestures"); *Plum Review* ("Wife of a Resident Alien"); *Southern Humanities Review* ("Sixth Anniversary"); *West Branch* ("Eve's Curse," "Ghost," "Onion, Fruit of Grace," "A Pass," "Sinning," "Thinking of Certain Mennonite Women," and "Word to Measure Space"); *Yarrow* ("Letter to Timothy Russell from Lewisburg").

"Flying Lesson" was published in *The Limits of Perfection*, ed. Rod Sawatsky and Scott Holland (Waterloo, Ontario: Institute of Anabaptist and Mennonite Studies, 1993). "Migraines" was published in *Father Poems*, ed. Elovic et al. (Brooklyn, N.Y.: Poetlink, 1995). "How My Father Learned English" will appear in *Learning by Heart*, ed. David Hassler and Maggie Anderson (University of Iowa Press, forthcoming).

"Lymphoma" is dedicated to Darcy Lynn; "To Honor the Dead" is dedicated to the memory of Jerome Badanes (1937–1995); "How It Looks from South Brooklyn" is for Robert Detweiler; "Houseguest Confession" is for John D. Rempel; "Brooklyn Bridge Showing Painters on Suspenders, 1914" honors Rudy Wiebe's sixtieth birthday; "Boustrophedon" is dedicated to the memory of Warren Rohrer (1927–1995); "Eve's Curse" is for Rebecca Ebersole; "Thinking of Certain Menno- nite Women" is for Lois Frey and Julie Musselman; "First Bird" marked the 1996 presidential inauguration of Shirley Hershey Showalter at Goshen College; "Flying Lesson" is dedicated to J. L. Burkholder.

The author thanks Blue Mountain Center, Ragdale Founda- tion, and Yaddo for residencies that assisted in the completion of this book and also thanks to Maggie Anderson, Donald Antrim, Jeff Gundy, Kathryn Maris, Susan Wheeler, and Melanie Zuercher for generously reading earlier versions of this manuscript.

photo by Carol Shadford

Julia Kasdorf grew up in western Pennsylvania and was educated at Goshen College and New York University, where she completed advanced studies in creative writing and English education. Her previous collection, *Sleeping Preacher*, won the 1991 Agnes Lynch Starrett Prize and the 1993 Great Lakes Colleges Association Award for New Writing. Her poems have appeared in *The New Yorker, Poetry*, and various anthologies and journals. She teaches at Messiah College and lives in Camp Hill, Pennsylvania.

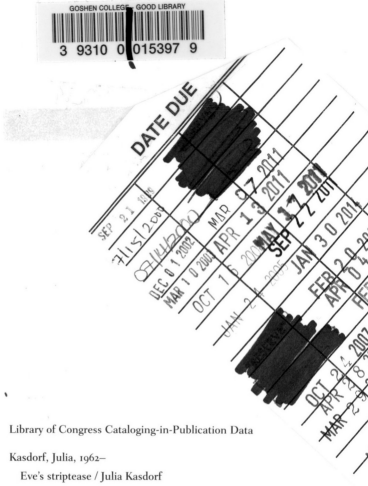

Library of Congress Cataloging-in-Publication Data

Kasdorf, Julia, 1962–
    Eve's striptease / Julia Kasdorf
        p.   cm. — (Pitt poetry series)
    ISBN 0-8229-4064-7 (acid-free paper). —
ISBN 0-8229-5668-3 (pbk. : acid-free paper)
    I. Title. II. Series.
PS3561.A6958E94   1997
811'.54—dc21   97-33956